A Complete Guide To
A Fundraising Opportunity

For Libraries
&
Other Organizations
Large & Small

Annette Chaudet

Cover Design: Antelope Design
Published by Pronghorn Press

www.pronghornpress.org

This Book is dedicated to those who continue, often against great odds, to promote the Arts through community involvement.

Table of Contents

Community Support.....71

Sponsors.....77

The Artists.....105

Recommended Materials.....127

Welcome to
Art of the Books!

Welcome to Art of the Books! You are about to embark on an exciting adventure full of possibilities and potential for your Library or other Arts-oriented organization. Because this project has so many parts, I would suggest that you read the book all the way through so you can understand how many different aspects there are to be considered and which may work best for your particular group. Good Luck!

A Fundraising Opportunity

Why Art of the Books?

Art of the Books is a project conceived as a fundraiser for Libraries and other organizations across the country. It is predicated on the many events featuring the large, artist embellished fiberglass animals that have been displayed in many states such as *Cows on Parade* in Chicago, *A Horse of Course* in Billings, Montana, *Where the Buffalo Roam* in Casper, Wyoming and *Trail of the Painted Ponies* in Santa Fe, New Mexico.

While this book focuses on the Art of the Books

project and the fiberglass book form, the principles can be applied to any project with a common object that can be embellished by artists

I am the publisher of a small press in Wyoming and, as an artist, I've participated in the Billings *Horse of Course* project and *Big Horn Magic* project in Billings, and *Where the Buffalo Roam* in Casper, both fundraisers with artists embellishing lifesize fiberglass animals which were sponsored by local businesses. After a summer of being "on the street" and viewed by locals and tourists alike, the animals were auctioned off and raised a great deal of money for their sponsoring organizations. As an example, Casper did thirty Buffalo along with one hundred small (9"-ish) flat cut steel buffalo and the sale of the pieces both large and small raised over a half million dollars!

The problems with this type of a project for libraries and smaller organizations are the cost of the large animals (approximately $1,500 to $2,000), the extra costs involved with their delivery to the organization as well as to and back from the artists, and then on to the coating facility, to the sponsor location and finally back to the auction. The animals take up a great deal of workspace while being embellished and also require a considerable amount of materials due to the large amount of surface area, another consideration for participating Artists.

Of course the buyers of the large pieces face the same dilemma when taking their pieces home! All these expenses—except, of course, those of the buyers—contribute to the high cost of sponsorships, which in turn can put such projects beyond the reach of smaller organizations who may have limited pools of both sponsors and buyers.

Artists in many of these large animal projects are also sometimes given stipends to help cover the costs of materials, paint and so forth—$400-$1,000 that was covered by the sponsorships—I think it's easy to see why the large outdoor pieces require a sizable sponsorship commitment.

These problems alone can make such a project daunting for smaller organizations but then when you add the expense of the concrete bases that have to be made for the large animals, the auto clear coating process that is required to protect the pieces destined to spend five months outdoors, many interested groups can become discouraged.

A Fundraising Opportunity

The Art of the Books pieces are intended to be displayed INSIDE the sponsoring businesses (though it is suggested they be viewable from outside) or at a single location such as a museum, large library or community space that would have suitable hours for public viewing. While it is possible to clear coat and display these pieces out of doors, vandalism might prove a problem because of the smaller size.

Also, these books require much less commitment—spacewise and timewise—from the Artists so it is easier for them to participate without a stipend for materials, another savings for the organization and their sponsors.

The Books

A Fundraising Opportunity

The Fiberglass Books

The actual Book is a three dimensional, hollow fiberglass cast in the form of an open book that measures 20" x 31" x 6" and weighs approximately fourteen pounds. It comes with a grey primer coat which makes a good base for your Artists to work on.

The Book is finished on all sides and can be displayed by hanging it on the wall (with the addition of a hanger), placing it in a bookstand so that both front and back can be seen or it can lay flat on a table like a real book. This gives your Artists the option of finishing all

A Fundraising Opportunity

four sides and inventing their own display options.

Of course, you can request that your Artists finish the Book in a particular way if you want a uniform presentation—say all hanging—though I would suggest that you let your Artists design the Book presentation in any way they see fit.

The Book was designed for and is exclusively produced by Fiberstock, Inc., one of the major producers of the fiberglass animals used around the country. They are wonderful people to work with and make a superior product. You can visit their website at *fiberstock.com* and see a picture of the Book. You can also explore some of the other city animal projects on their website.

This Book form solves all the problems enumerated in the previous section. It is small enough and light weight enough to ship in a box, via UPS, and the cost of the piece is $300 versus the cost of the larger animals.

The small, secondary piece is a custom produced papier maché open Book form, handmade in Indonesia, that measures 13.3" x 10.5" x 2.5". It is also two sided so can be displayed in the same way as the large Book; hanging, in a stand or laying flat. These Books will be available through Art of the Books at *artofthebooks.com* and these will be your supplementary pieces for your silent auction.

Projects of thirty to forty of the large animals have generally had about one hundred small pieces for their silent auctions. In communities too small to support an auction of the large Books and who consequently only do a few of the large pieces, the small Books in a silent auction can be a significant addition to the revenues from three to four large Books. Even the smallest venue should be able to support at least twenty-five of the small Books in addition to the larger ones.

As both the fiberglass and the papier maché pieces are pieces are handmade, one piece at a time, I must caution you to allow enough time for production and not to order late and hope for early delivery. Both suppliers will be able to give you projected delivery dates when you order but production time will generally be in the ninety days range.

A Fundraising Opportunity

Before You Begin...

A Fundraising Opportunity

Who and What

You need committed volunteers and a Project Coordinator. This type of project, while being rewarding and sometimes offering astonishing results, requires a good block of time and effort. Some of the duties of your Project Coordinator will be:

    1. To determine the philosophy of
       the project.

A Fundraising Opportunity

2. Recruit committee chairmen.

3. To develop and implement plan
   for obtaining project Sponsors.

4. To collaborate with committee
   chairmen to develop committee
   job descriptions.

5. To collaborate with committee
   chairmen to develop a project budget.

6. To collaborate with committee
   chairmen to develop a project timeline.

7. To plan for Sponsor recognition
   throughout project.

8. To provide support for committee
   chairmen as needed.

9. To determine the need for contracts
   and insurance for the project.

ART OF THE BOOKS

You also need to decide on a name for your project. You can go with Art of the Books and just leave it wide open to your Artists' interpretations or you can be more specific and choose something like "Childhood Dreams," "The World of Books," "Words of Wisdom," "Read All About It"or perhaps something that might be specific to your location like "Gifts from the Sea" or "Desert Wisdom."

Any catchy or alliterative theme that will stick in the minds of the public can be helpful in spreading the word. And remember you can use Art of the Books and have a specific theme as a subtitle such as "Art of the Books: A Thousand Dreams."

A Fundraising Opportunity

Getting Started

A Fundraising Opportunity

Give Yourself a
Mission Statement!

    A mission statement for your project will help you keep your priorities in order and make it easier to talk about the project with potential donors and sponsors. Often people will ask you to tell them something about your project and your mission statement allows you to give them a simple answer. You can always tell them more.

Make sure your mission statement suits your situation. Here's an example:

The Joys of Childhood
Art of the Books Project

This project is undertaken to:

Provide revenue to complete refurbishing of the children's library at the Emerald City Public Library and to fund an expanded summer reading program through community involvement with an arts based fundraising project.

While that is a somewhat simplistic example, I do encourage you to keep your mission statement as simple as possible. It will make it much easier to keep your focus and to talk to people about what it is that you're doing.

Deciding on the
Size of Your Project

The size of your project will be governed primarily by the potential number of Sponsors you are able to bring on board. Another important consideration is who you will be selling the Books to at the final auction.

Don't let these considerations deflate your ambitions. Perhaps you are a small library in a location not exactly brimming with potential buyers. If that's the case, you will have to consider raising your sponsorship prices so that the Books can either be sold at lower prices which won't effect your monetary goals, or perhaps the Books will remain unsold and merely be displayed at your library or make the rounds of the schools and other businesses in your community. We will discuss this more in the section on Sponsors.

First you will need a Project Coordinator, someone to oversee all the aspects and keep an eye both on the budget and the calendar. For larger projects this person will oversee the various committees and coordinate their efforts and keep them on track.

One of the things that has been expressed by past groups is that the director's job is very time consuming on projects of twenty-five pieces and up and therefore it has been suggested that this should be a paid position. This is, of course, a decision you will have to make for yourselves. (*See the Committees section for a complete list of the Coordinator's responsibilities and descriptions of the duties of each Committee.)

You will need to decide which of the Committees apply to your project. This, like everything else, will depend on the size of your undertaking.

Think about the Committees, determine how many volunteers you'll need for each and what their duties will be. When you start asking for help, you want to be able to be very clear about what you are asking people to do. They are much more likely to agree to help you if they know exactly what it is you want from them.

A Fundraising Opportunity

Developing a
Preliminary Budget

In order to be able to decide on what to charge for Sponsorships for your Books you will need to develop a rough budget. This will, again, depend on the size of your project, but even the smallest will need a budget to work from.

The following is an Income and Expense sheet for a project of the large animals that involved thirty-two large pieces and one hundred small pieces. The auction was a sit-down dinner for eight hundred and included phone bidders. While the auction numbers are probably far higher than you can expect on the Book pieces, it will give you some idea of the events and considerations for a project that size:

ART OF THE BOOKS

INCOME

Large Piece Sponsorships	$ 91,600.
Extra group sponsorships (individuals who grouped together to sponsor)	$ 6,500.
"Other Sponsors" (This is in kind donations for specific things such as the catalogue)	$ 27,863.
Event "Dollars" (Coupons for mdse.)	$ 3,200.
Donations	$ 2,440.
Live Auction	$293,500.
Silent Auction (the small pieces)	$ 33,580.
Auction Ticket sales	$ 52,945
Raffle (this was for a smaller "young" animal)	$ 3,773.
Sales of Merchandise	$107,334.
TOTAL INCOME:	$622,906.

A Fundraising Opportunity

EXPENSES:

Paid Ads	$ 3,005.
Raffle Tickets printing	$ 250.
Receptions	$ 782.
Kick Off Party	$ 334.
Clear Coating	$ 595.
Large Animals (purchase)	$ 33,613.
Signage (banners & name plates)	$ 589.
Auction Invites & Postage	$ 1,330.
Misc. Postage & Supplies	$ 4,469.
Auction Dinner Food	$ 17,510.
Auctioneer (Percentage)	$ 14,835.
100 Small Animal Pieces (for Silent Auction)	$ 949.
Credit Card Fees (%)	$ 3,317.
Phone Lines & Internet	$ 752.
Auction programs + Bid Cards	$ 489.
Wine	$ 2,613.
Storage	$ 854.
Repairs to Animals + Security	$ 882.
Artist's Stipends	$ 25,600.

ART OF THE BOOKS

Artist's Auction Dinners	$	1,480.
Brochures	$	3,240.
Cost of Merchandise	$	39,160.
Layout & TV Production (Commercial)	$	1,500.
TOTAL EXPENSES	$	160,734.
NET PROFIT	$	462,172.

There were also "in kind" Donations totalling just over $33,000 that included all or partial donations of things like Photography, Printing, Newspaper Advertising, Food, Concrete, Clear Coating, Transportation of the pieces and so forth.

When you are making your preliminary budget consider which things you can hope to find sponsors for beyond the actual Books. In the budget above there was a single donor who paid for all of the small animal pieces for the silent auction.

A Fundraising Opportunity

ART of the BOOKS

A Project Timeline

Basically the Art of the Books project spreads over fourteen months. That will take you from deciding you want to do it to the final accounting.

If you are in a part of the country that has a very popular season/tourist time, you might want to adapt the schedule as this one is designed to take advantage of summer tourism. If you are in Florida in an area where the snowbirds flock, you may want to change the schedule. The same applies to a library in a ski area where winter sports may dictate the most popular time for community involvement. You will have to decide what works best for you and for your community.

So, based on a standard summer event with an auction in the fall, this is how your schedule might look:

March-June

Finalize your mission statement.

Begin discussions and explore possibilities.

Research similar projects in other cities for additional ideas as well as inspiration, such as *Cows On Parade* in Chicago, *Trail of the Painted Ponies* in Santa Fe, *Horse of Course* in Billings, Montana, and *Where the Buffalo Roam* in Casper, Wyoming.

Start talking to people about the upcoming project. Be sure to let your Chamber of Commerce know your plans well in advance as it will prevent scheduling conflicts. Start a buzz, even if it's on a small scale.

Get your local newspaper involved. They will do a story for you and you can mention that you are looking for volunteers and sponsors. While this won't bring you all the folks you need it may bring a few your way that might not be on your lists!

Organize committees and develop a potential Sponsorship List. List groups beyond the regular Artists or organizations you might want to invite to do small Books. This could include schools, non-sponsoring businesses, service organizations and others who will not be the Artists receiving an invitation to participate with one of the large Books.

July-September

Recruit your Sponsors.

A Fundraising Opportunity

September

With Sponsors on board, issue your call for Artists.

Start lining up support commitments from food service, art and printing people, explore advertising options and any donated space, publicity or air time that might be available.

Explore grant and funding possibilities from your arts council, chamber of commerce, and travel and tourist councils.

October-November

Order big Books.

Notify selected Artists and invite those not selected to embellish a small Book.

December

Order small Books.

January

Large Books arrive in town.

Begin to line up publicity opportunities. Most magazines need materials two months in advance and if they want to do an article, they may want even more lead time. Be sure press releases go out beyond your immediate area so people in neighboring communities can begin to be interested.

February

Artists receive their large Books.

Plan dates for events. Remember to consider what other community events might be scheduled.

Consolidate plans for merchandise.

March

Small Books arrive and are distributed.

April

Artists complete embellishment of large Books and return them to you.

May

Photograph Books. Even if you are not going to produce a catalogue, you will want a record and you will need photos for publicity.

Artist and Sponsor preview party.

Small Books begin coming in.

ART OF THE BOOKS

Early June

Project commences! Kick-off celebration.

Books displayed around town, publicity campaign in high gear.

Labor Day

Pick up the Books from display locations.

September

Auction, raffle, celebration!

October

Final Thank Yous to Artists and Sponsors.

Finalize your accounting and close the books on your project.

A Fundraising Opportunity

Committees

A Fundraising Opportunity

A Coordinator for Your Project

First you will want to select a Project Coordinator whose duties will be as follows:

1. Help determine the philosophy of project.

2. Recruit committee chairmen.

3. Develop and implement a plan for obtaining project sponsors.

A Fundraising Opportunity

4. Collaborate with committee chairmen to develop committee job descriptions.

5. Collaborate with committee chairmen to develop a project budget.

6. Collaborate with committee chairmen to develop a project timeline.

7. Plan for Sponsor recognition throughout the project.

8. Provide support for committee chairmen as needed.

9. Determine need for contracts and insurance for your project.

I want to give you a list of the committees and what they do. This many committees would be for a large scale project and, obviously, smaller undertakings could combine these necessary functions. Take a look through this list and see how they might apply to your project.

Details Committee

The Details Committee will take care of the insurance policy for the art pieces. If your organization already carries insurance, it is possible that you can just have a rider for the duration of the project. The insurance should cover the cost of replacing one of the pieces and the artist's fee (if any). Your legal advisor can discuss the liability issues with you, but the Book pieces should require less liability coverage than the lifesize (and much heavier animals). Also, as the Books will not be displayed on the street, they should be less subject to vandalism. This will, in most cases, also allow you to forgo security coverage. You will have to adapt your insurance considerations to your specific needs.

Your Artist contract should provide for the Artist to repair any minor damage which will help if there are any small problems. Again, as the Books are not going to be out on the street twenty-four hours a day, they will be less subject to damage, but nicks and dings do happen so be sure your Artists are committed to small repairs or that you have someone else lined up who could do them.

The Details Committee will also be responsible for ordering the Books and being sure they arrive. This means both the large and small Books. They will manage the movement of the Books to the photographer, to any events where the Books appear, to the places where the Books will be displayed and then back to your auction or final event. These are the people who will be sure the Books travel safely.

You will find many other small duties you can assign to your Details Committee.

An Artists Committee

The Artists Committee will be responsible for all contact with the Artists. This will include contacting Artists, arranging to have the designs submitted, notifying the Artists you select to participate, and being available to the Artists who may have questions. This committee will see that the Artists are kept in the event loop, that the contracts are returned, that materials information gets to the Artists along with their pieces. And remember, you have the Artists for the large Books and the Artists for the small Books to deal with, though the smaller Books will require a lot less effort as you will not have such a big investment in those pieces and you won't need contracts.

Artists tend to be "right brained" so they will, no doubt, require some "wrangling" in that you will need to check in with them and be sure they are on time and will have their pieces completed on schedule. You will need to be sure the contracts are signed before they get their pieces and that they give you the information you will need about them and their piece for whatever publicity you plan.

There are more details of what the Artists Committee should do in the Artist section.

Special Events Committee

The need for this Committee is completely dependent on the number of events you plan. If you have a very full schedule of events with perhaps a Potential Sponsors Get Acquainted event, an Artist/Sponsor Party, a Kick Off Party, a Raffle of one of the pieces and any other events leading up to the auction or final event, you may want to make smaller Committees to handle some of them individually. Again, this completely depends on the size and number of your events and you will be able to judge what you need. Just remember that each event will require coordination and careful planning.

Merchandise Committee

This committee will handle all the work that's connected with creating, producing and promoting any merchandise that you want to have as a part of your project. This could include mugs, shirts, posters, a catalogue/book, postcards, bumper stickers—anything related to your particular project that you might be able to sell and make a profit on.

And there are good profits to be made in merchandising. You will want to find Sponsors who will

A Fundraising Opportunity

cover the production costs for the items or to spread those costs out over the costs of the Book sponsorships, or a combination of the two. While some items, such as a color catalogue or even a hard bound color book of your project can be very expensive to produce, you should be able to more than double your investment, which can result in a considerable amount of revenue.

ART OF THE BOOKS

Auction Committee

The auction committee will handle the technical and financial considerations for your auction.

Many groups have decided that there will be a minimum bid required for each piece and that seems to be in line with the actual cost of the piece plus any Artist's fee plus a little extra for good measure.

Two of the horse projects that I'm aware of had a $2,500 minimum bid and a $4,000 minimum bid respectively, the higher amount being in a large city that

A Fundraising Opportunity

did eighty horses and raised over a million dollars. Remember that your sponsorships should have covered your costs on each piece but you will still want to establish a minimum bid in keeping with the value of the art. This is something that you can talk to your auctioneers about if you feel you need guidance.

The Auction Committee and Event Committee may work together on the auction or the Event Committee may handle the actual event—food service, location, parking, etc.—while the Auction Committee will deal with only the auctioneers and the financial end. You will have to decide, based on the size of your event.

One of the interesting things I came across in my research is the fact that one group had decided that any pieces that didn't make their minimum auction bid would be sold on EBay. All their pieces sold, but it is certainly something you can consider. For those of you who have a very small undertaking, EBay might be a fun alternative to an auction event and would certainly provide you with access to a large number of potential buyers!

And regarding your buyers at the auction: In the events that I'm aware of, often buyers bought more than one piece. The most that I came across was a big city event where a car dealer bought six of the large animals for a considerable amount of money!

An additional note: Be careful about the order in which the pieces are auctioned. Things tend to start slow until the auction gets going. One group went from "Good" to "Less Popular" to "Good" and saved the "Best" for last.

A Fundraising Opportunity

Publicity Committee

This Committee will be on top of keeping the event in the public eye. They will be in charge of arranging all the publicity from media coverage to brochures and handouts.

As suggested in the Publicity section, you will want to see if you can have coverage every week in the paper, on the radio and, in some places, television may also be an option. You will find that your event will "sell itself" if you have done your "early buzz" groundwork.

A Fundraising Opportunity

You probably already have a website and this should be included in the work of the Publicity Committee. Your website should have information about your project including pictures of your Books when you have them as well as where they can be seen. Information about your Artists and Sponsors should also be on your website. You will want to offer your merchandise and have a calendar of events. People want a place where they can keep abreast of your project.

The Publicity Committee should also be responsible for getting the pieces photographed when they are done. All your media will want pictures and even if you don't do a catalogue or book, you want to be sure that you have a professional photographic record of each piece.

Sponsors Committee

This Committee will be responsible for finding Sponsors and will also track the Sponsorship Contracts, take good care of the Sponsors and be the contact for the Sponsors if they have any questions or need any help.

The Committee will be sure that the relationship between the organization and the Sponsor is a warm one that lets the Sponsors feel they are valued.

A Fundraising Opportunity

Community Support

A Fundraising Opportunity

ART OF THE BOOKS

Getting Your Community
Excited About Your Project

Once you decide to go ahead with your project, you should immediately begin to focus on gaining the support of your community. Arrange for interviews with the local papers, the radio stations and you should be able to interest your local TV station in your efforts. Always remember to mention that you will be seeking sponsors and volunteers as well as interested artists.

A Fundraising Opportunity

Focus on how the events connected with the project will benefit your area; maybe it will be an added attraction for tourists, maybe it will tie in to other summer events, perhaps you are going to draw attention to a particular area of the city where other events are getting underway.

Be sure to use your mission statement when you do your interviews and talk about why you've chosen this project, what it will do for your organization and how that will benefit the community in general. Remember, your project was undertaken to provide revenue for your specific need, but also to provide a means to showcase public art, to promote a sense of community pride and to bring to public consciousness your library or organization as a community resource.

Even though this is an early stage, you should be able to talk about some of the events that you hope to have in conjunction with your project, and other groups that you hope might be interested in coordinating with you. This will get people thinking about how they can contribute or combine the timing of their events with yours. It will be early enough to draw you all together so that you can make your project even more.

ART OF THE BOOKS

As you move farther along your timeline, be sure to keep the community involved. See how you can work with your travel/tourism council, your chamber of commerce—any of the business associations where you have sponsors may want to be involved.

If you have a museum, gallery space, community center or any similar public place, you might consider doing a Kick Off party there. You could begin with a private Artist/Sponsor party. Another event you could hold before the Books move to their sponsor locations might be a wine tasting, a tapas party, a writer's reading and book signing, a poetry reading—something to which you can sell tickets for additional fundraising and which is an opportunity for the pieces to be exhibited all together in one location. Perhaps this event would raise the money to print your posters or go toward producing the catalogue.

A Fundraising Opportunity

Sponsors

A Fundraising Opportunity

Deciding on
the Cost of Sponsorship

The things to consider when deciding on the cost of sponsorship will depend on your budget and the size of your project.

For the large Books, ideally you will have one Sponsor per Book but this will depend on the size and affluence of your community. To figure the cost of sponsorship, you must begin with the cost of the large

A Fundraising Opportunity

Book, of course, and the cost of the shipping to you. Then add an average shipping cost to and from the Artist if you anticipate that will be a consideration. (If you have enough Artists close at hand, they may pick up and deliver the Books themselves.)

You need to add in costs of any merchandise you want to produce for which you don't have separate Sponsors. You may also combine the two, having specific merchandise Sponsors who will pay only part of the cost of production because it is supplemented by an amount coming from each of the Book sponsorships.

Part of the merchandise costs can come from other donations and sponsorships from various businesses or patrons but you need to look at all the costs of planned events, advertising and promotional materials, postage for invitations and announcements, etc. before you start figuring out the cost of a sponsorship.

If you have a small event and don't feel that your auction prices will be very sizable, or if you are very small and perhaps only doing three to four Books and don't feel that a final auction will work for you, you will want to include an additional amount in the sponsorships so that your profit comes from the actual sponsorships rather than from auction sales. In this case you will have to consider what will happen to the Books at the end of

ART OF THE BOOKS

the display period. Perhaps they will go to a community location or be displayed in your library. Or you might choose the EBay option for additional fundraising. You can get the community behind this and they can track the EBay auction.

You also may need to include the cost of some of the small Books or at least consider the cost of how many you want to do. You may be able to find a single sponsor to cover the cost of all the small Books or you may split the cost among two or three Sponsors.

You need to add the cost of the signs or title cards that will go with each piece. For small projects these can be hand done calligraphy or computer generated, for larger projects you might want to have engraved or silk screened metal. The larger signs on some of the animal projects were made by trophy companies who may be able to give you some suitable options. The signage should be large enough to be easily read, should list the title of the piece, the Artist and the Sponsor.

So, at a minimum, the cost of a large Book sponsorship needs to cover:

1. The cost of the fiberglass Book.

A Fundraising Opportunity

2. All shipping costs, including those
   to and from the artists.
   * Some artists will both pick up and
   deliver their piece in person but you
   should include the cost just to cover
   yourself. Anything you save in
   another way means more profit
   for your project.

3. The artist's stipend, should you choose to
   give one.

4. An estimated percentage of the
   photography costs, if you can't get
   them donated.

5. A percentage of the cost of promotion.
   * All your promotion costs should not
   come from these sponsorships but
   you should include some money to
   help out where your donations may
   fall short of what you need. Again
   this all depends on the scope of your
   undertaking.

Remember: If you are a very small group and don't anticipate being able to auction your pieces, then you may consider raising your sponsorship cost much higher, to say $1,000 or $1,500 or more, as this is where your money will come from. This is not an unreasonable cost for sponsorship for a large project but for a small library undertaking five Books or less it may seem like a lot! If you are small and don't think your Sponsors could afford this sort of cost, you can allow two or three businesses to sponsor a piece. (see Finding Sponsors) You might also consider having the whole community contribute and see how much money and consequently how many books you can support. You could still have grouped businesses or schools support several books and then the community as a whole support a few more.

And keep in mind that you will be contracting your Sponsors months in advance of the kick off for your event so it can be an added incentive if their cost of sponsorship can be spread over several payments. Just be sure you have the full amount before their piece goes to an Artist!

A Fundraising Opportunity

Finding Sponsors

Finding your Sponsors is the biggest challenge you will face but it can also be both fun and rewarding for you *and* for the Sponsors. If you are following your timeline, you will have put out the initial announcements to create a buzz. These are most likely newspaper articles and radio announcements about your project and what you hope to accomplish. You mentioned that interested Artists, Sponsors and Volunteers should contact you and with luck you have some names. You will pick up a few early people this way but remember: you will have to get some folks to help you who will get out there and "sell" the idea to your potential Sponsors.

You can begin this process with a letter to as many people as you think have promise. And work the long shots. You never know who might be looking for a promotional opportunity.

Since the Books will not be out "on the street" as the larger animals sometimes are, they will be displayed inside the sponsoring business. You may want to include something in the Sponsorship Agreement that says they will be displayed in such a way that they can be seen from outside the business, such as in a window.

Perhaps all the Books will be displayed at a single location such as a gallery, museum, library or community center. What's important is that if people come to town to see the Books, they need to be easily accessible. You can decide how best to make this happen within the parameters of your Sponsors and your community.

No matter how small your community, you will be able to find Sponsors. There will be businesses and perhaps even a few generous patrons who will want to participate. Sometimes you can get a service group, school or class, or several individuals to sponsor a piece.

One of the large animal projects with a $2,500 sponsorship cost had two groups of twenty-five people who came together, named themselves and each contributed $100 toward the sponsorship!

Don't limit your potential Sponsors list to retail, high visibility businesses. Consider banks, lumber yards or hardware stores, realtors, lawyers, insurance people—people who depend on your patrons for their businesses. Don't forget your building services people: contractors, plumbers, painters. Even in an economically depressed area, several small businesses might go together to support your efforts. And don't forget the energy suppliers for your community.

In larger communities you will have many potential Sponsors to choose from. Look to the largest employers who might well decide to sponsor more than one Book. You may be able to choose first from your arts related businesses such as bookstores and galleries. Make a list of your "dream sponsors" and then go in descending order. If you are working in a particular area or to promote a location or particular event, think of the sponsors closest in location or type of businesses.

Remember that you may want to tap your food service people such as restaurants, grocers and caterers and the liquor stores and bottlers for your events, so I

A Fundraising Opportunity

would suggest holding them in reserve until you have a handle on what you will need. The same goes for companies who might produce some of your merchandise such as the screen printers or traditional printers, embroidery companies and so forth. You may allow them sponsorship on an "in kind" donation basis.

Make Yourself a List

Large libraries probably have a number of generous and willing supporters who will be a tremendous help to them throughout the duration of the event. I would suggest that individuals be put on a separate list and that you begin with local businesses.

Depending on where you feel most likely to find support, start with businesses in areas where the public would be likely to view the pieces. This may be in a downtown area, an area that is being revitalized, or a large shopping mall—the Sponsors in these areas who would be anxious to have a piece at their business as it will bring in potential customers. (*See What's In It For Them?)

It could be in a community center or a museum if you aren't displaying the pieces in individual businesses. No matter where the pieces will be on display, you want to be sure that it is easy for the public to view them. If they are going to be inside businesses, they should be easily visible from outside, such as in a window. Your community and its particular dynamic will tell you what areas will work best for you.

You should also be able to get support from the biggest employers in your town though they may not be a business that would have a Book on display at their offices. As examples—a lumber company, tire factory or bottling company may be a big employer in your area. They may not have their offices in a location suited to public viewing, but they might be very willing to become a Sponsor for a piece in a high profile location.

Sometimes a school will take on a Sponsorship along with the embellishment where the students will raise money for the cost and will get together to decide how they want to embellish their piece. The students enjoy seeing their piece at a high profile location where

ART OF THE BOOKS

the whole community can admire their work and parents, teachers and students have become involved. That's a lot of folks talking about your project and spreading the word and the excitement! One of these pieces done by a school was a colt in one of the horse projects. The piece then was raffled off and raised even more money.

Your retail merchants will be strong supporters but don't forget doctors and lawyers, service organizations, and banks.

And if you are a very small community or if you are having trouble finding Sponsors for your last few pieces, you might run something in the paper encouraging groups of individuals to get together and sponsor a piece. Perhaps the Red Hat ladies or Soccer Moms or maybe the tenants of an office building. You know your own community and I'm sure you will have lots of ideas. What's important is for your Sponsors to feel that they are a part of a very important and exciting event.

A Fundraising Opportunity

What's In It For Them?

It's a perfectly fair question and one you can expect will be asked. The simple answer is support and exposure. Depending on your community, the size of your project and the number of pieces you are presenting, the Sponsors should be assured that their names will be prominent throughout the duration of your event. This means that the public will be aware of them and their business over a period of approximately ten months. They should be included in everything that

A Fundraising Opportunity

you do.

Newspaper articles should feature different Sponsors in stories about your project and why they decided to become Sponsors. Their names should be included in all publicity including any maps, brochures and the catalogue, if you decide to do one. Their name will be on the signage on the individual piece. They will be invited to the Sponsor/Artist preview which is the first time all the pieces will be seen together before they are distributed to the locations where they will be on display. This will also give them the opportunity to meet the Artist who created their piece.

Your Sponsors should have two free tickets to the Auction and other fundraising events. They should get a copy of the catalogue, if you do one. If you print postcards of the piece, your Sponsors should have a number of cards for their own use. Any things you can do for them to let them know how much you value them is a perk for them.

Check with your legal advisor and see what the tax advantages for your Sponsors will be. Sponsorships should qualify as tax deductible donations.

A Sample Sponsorship Agreement

The following agreement is a sample sponsorship contract. YOU MUST run it by your legal advisor to be sure that it addresses points specific to your project and also to BE SURE it conforms to the laws of YOUR state, YOUR organization and its legal concerns. It is offered here to ONLY demonstrate points you need to consider. And I would suggest that the agreement be as brief and concise as possible.

Your legal advisor will also be able to tell you how much of the sponsorships might be tax deductible for your Sponsors.

AGREEMENT

Thank you for joining as a Site Sponsor for *The Art of the Books* project of the *Emerald City Library* in support of the fundraising initiative *to renovate the Children's Library and support the Summer Reading program.* Your sponsorship and provision of a location to display one of the Books adds great excitement and is critical to the success of our efforts.

Here's what Art of the Books provides:

> 1. Moving the Book to your site between May 29 and June 1.

> 2. A sponsorship plaque identifying the project Sponsor, the art Book title, and

name of the artist.

3. Maps and map holders all around town identifying all the Book locations, as well as their sponsors.

4. Name and telephone number of the project contact, and an alternate.

The *Art of the Books* project of the *Emerald City Library*, a non-profit organization, accepts responsibility for any damage to the physical Book and holds the Site Sponsor harmless for damage to the Book which is not caused by the willful negligence of the Site Sponsor

Here's what we expect of you:

1. Display area which is prominent, and easily viewable by the public.

2. Display area kept free of debris and obstructions.

3. Display area which is well-lit, with all-night illumination.

A Fundraising Opportunity

Assurance that you, the exhibiting Site Sponsor, have adequate public liability insurance covering the premises. (Please consult with your insurer about the need for a "rider" on your policy naming *Emerald City Library* as an additional insured for the duration of the display period.)

Report, as you would any unusual activity, safety or security breach, to the Emerald City Police Department.

If you have questions or concerns, call your project contact:
(Names of Co-Chairs and phone numbers)

By signing this agreement, the Site Sponsor, to the fullest extent permitted by law, expressly agrees and understands that it shall indemnify, defend and hold harmless the *Art of the Books* project and *the Emerald City Library*, from any and all claims for bodily injury, personal injury and property damage arising out of the sole negligence of the Site Sponsor. The Site Sponsor will purchase and maintain commercial general liability insurance naming the *Emerald City Library*, as an additional insured.

ART OF THE BOOKS

The Art of the Books Committee is most grateful for your generous sponsorship of this project and your display of the fabulous art in your business.

On this _____ day of _____, 2005 the undersigned enter into this Agreement.

_____

Site Sponsor

By _____

Authorized Sponsor Site Representative

the Emerald City Library

By_____

_____

Position Title

A Fundraising Opportunity

Who Gets Which Book?

This is a big question and fortunately for you, experience has provided a precise answer: The Committee will decide which Book goes where. If you let the Sponsors choose from the completed pieces, a number of them will end up wanting the same piece which means other pieces will be wallflowers and you will end up with unhappy Sponsors who feel their piece is not what they wanted. It has been proven again and again that when the piece is chosen *for* the Sponsor, they are inevitably very pleased and tend to feel that they got lucky and got the best piece. I'm not sure what the logic here is, but trust me when I tell you this *IS* the only viable solution to keep everyone happy.

As far as the Committee is concerned, they will find that selecting the locations for the finished pieces can be fun. Matching Sponsor to piece can be a challenge but you may find that your finished pieces often seem "custom made" for certain Sponsors. And you will have an idea when the Selection Committee is reviewing the Artists' design submissions as to which pieces may be uniquely suited to particular Sponsors. As an example, the piece I did for *Where the Buffalo Roam* was a play on words for "Buffalo Robe" and the buffalo was wearing a bathrobe with a child-like buffalo print. It went to a children's dentist and was a big hit with the patients, especially because I had painted smiling teeth on the buffalo that could only be seen by sitting on the ground and looking up at his mouth!

ART OF THE BOOKS

A Fundraising Opportunity

The Artists

A Fundraising Opportunity

Remember...

Without your Artists you have no project. Always remember to treat them with respect and appreciation. These are talented people giving generously of their time, talent and money to help your organization. Be sure to let them know that you value them.

A Fundraising Opportunity

An Artists Committee

There is a lot to be done on the Artist side of things and you may want a separate Committee to deal with them. Regardless of the size of your project, these things will need to be addressed:

1. Plan and implement an "Artists call" which will involve both publicity and individual letters to Artists whom you would like to see participate.

2. Develop standards for Artists' design submissions. This information will be included in your "invitation to participate" letter to Artists which will go out to the Artists on your list as well as to those Artists who contact you and want to participate. You should include a drawing of the Book that the Artists can use for their design which will give you a uniform set of artwork to judge and make your selections from.

3. Designate a Selection Committee for Artist selection who will make the final choice from submitted designs.

4. Provide contracts for Artists selected to participate.

5. Determine the amount of Artists' stipends if you feel you would like to provide them (on a piece this size I would say it it is not strictly necessary) and facilitate payment. Remember this cost needs to be included in sponsorship costs if you decide to provide it. The Artists should be paid when they return the finished piece.

6. Develop Artist recognition plans. This might

include studio tours, and artists featured in the local media throughout the term of the project. It will include inviting the Artists to the Artist/Sponsor preview party and should include free admission to all related events for the Artist and one guest. This includes your final auction event. People at all events will be interested in meeting and talking to the artists and it is to your advantage to include them as much as possible.

7. Facilitate and Coordinate the embellishment of the project Books. This means providing your Artists with all information about materials that are known to be compatible with the fiberglass Books as well as being sure the Books get to the Artists and back to you when they are completed. (Your Details Committee may handle this.) You will be the contact for your Artists should they have any questions about anything.

8. Find photographer to photograph Books for use on print materials and merchandise. Often you can find someone willing to provide this service in exchange for the publicity and perhaps samples of everything on which their work appears. Others may make a partial donation of their service costs. It is important that you have someone who is experienced in commercial

photography and will provide good quality photos. They should have lights and a studio setup where the pieces can be photographed to best advantage. As the Books are not as large as the animals, you may be able to provide a photography space at your location.

9. Collaborate with the Details Committee on signage, site selection, and Book repair plans.

10. Collaborate with the Media Committee to develop all print material including brochures, posters, note cards and books. This means that you will also collect bio information from all your Artists which will help with all aspects of publicity, including production of a catalogue if you decide to produce one.

11. Recruit committee volunteers as needed.

How to Find Your Artists

It is easy to find a good number of Artists who are excited about participating in your project. Depending on the number of Books you want to do, you can invite your Artists individually, put out an open call for design submissions, or both. You may have received some names in response to your early buzz newspaper and radio coverage.

Because the Books can be shipped via UPS, you can go outside your immediate area for your Artists if you choose to. Even if you are in a small community, you no doubt have some Artists close by. And large project or small, don't hesitate to contact very well known artists. You will be surprised how many of them might be willing to help you and a big name is always a draw for your auction buyers.

But if you don't have an Artist list to draw from, you can contact galleries, your state or community arts council or other arts organizations and offer the opportunity for artists to submit designs. You will then be able to choose the most suitable designs for your project.

The fiberglass Book has been designed to be much smaller and more easily transported than the life size animals for many of the reasons I have mentioned before. You should, of course, pay any transportation costs of the piece to the artist and the return of the finished piece, though you will find that most Artists will decide to personally deliver their work to avoid damage. When an Artist is contracted to participate, you will be able to find out their needs in advance.

From an Artist's point of view, I don't feel that with the Book it is necessary to offer materials compensation to those Artists you select to participate.

ART OF THE BOOKS

The large animals require a huge amount of materials which can be quite costly but the Books are a manageable size and also don't require a big commitment of floorspace while being embellished.

In a bigger venue the Artist stipend is a courtesy and can be considered, especially if your final auction sales prices are expected to be quite high. Some projects have allowed the Artists ten percent of the final sales price, which is bound to please the Artist. If you can afford to do it, it is added incentive for the Artist and some of them may choose to donate their stipend or their auction percentage back to your project!

A Fundraising Opportunity

What You Need From Your Artists

You will want a brief biography from your Artists that you can use for publicity and also for a catalogue, if you decide to do one. This should contain some information about them and their careers but should also address the reason that they wanted to participate in your project and something related to the inspiration for their piece.

You must have a contract with your Artists. This

needs to be signed in advance of them receiving their piece. I have included a sample but, as with the Sponsorship Agreement, *you must obtain the advice of a lawyer as to how it might apply to your organization and the governing laws in your state.* You should *use the sample only as a guide* to the points that should be considered.

A Sample Artist Agreement

Agreement for the Design and Implication of an Art Book Piece for the Emerald City Art of the Books Project.

This agreement is entered into this ___day of ___ 2005 between the Emerald City Library, (ECL) and _____(Artist)

A Fundraising Opportunity

Recitals

The ECL plans to host a public Art exhibition in the Summer 2006 titled Art of the Books for the purpose of supporting the renovation of the ECL Children's Library and the Summer Reading Program, public art and holding a public auction of the art pieces on September 12, 2006.

The ECL desires that the Artist submit a certain work of art based on the fiberglass Book sculpture provided to the Artist by the ECL.

Therefore, the ECL and Artist agree as follows:

1. The Artist, without compensation, has provided a design for the Book art piece which has been selected by the ECL for inclusion in the Art of the Books event above described.

2. The Artist warrants that

A. the submitted design is unique and original and a product of the Artist's own creative efforts.

B. The Art of the Books piece is one of a kind created exclusively for the ECL Art of the Books Project.

C. The design and the executed piece are free of any and all lien claims.

D. The Artist fully understands and agrees that the Artist is not an employee of the ECL and is retained as an independent contractor to the ECL and has no right to assume or create any legal obligation on behalf of the ECL.

3. The ECL has accepted the Art of the Books design provided by the Artist and on or about March 1, 2006 will provide the Artist with the fiberglass Book sculpture that is the base for their design.

4. The finished Art Piece must be embellished to conform with the approved design. If, in the reasonable judgement of the ECL the completed piece deviates substantially from the approved design, the ECL may withhold display of the finished piece.

5. The Artist is responsible for all loss or damage

to the piece from the time the Artist takes possession of the Book sculpture until it is returned to and accepted by the ECL.

6. The Artist recognizes that time is of the essence and must perform under the terms of this agreement in such a manner as to complete their work by May, 15, 2006.

7. The artist agrees to make any necessary minor repairs at the request of the ECL that might be needed on the piece before the auction on September 12, 2006. The parties agree that such repairs may be necessary after several months during which the piece will be on public display. The Artist WILL NOT be responsible for repairs of damage caused by others and will be compensated for such repairs should they become necessary.

8. The Artist must defend, indemnify and hold harmless ECL and its agents, directors, and employees against all suits, claims, damages, losses and expenses, including attorney's fees, caused by, growing out of or incidental to the performance of this Agreement by the Artist or subcontractors of the Artist, if any, to the full extent allowed by law and not beyond any extent which

render these provisions void or unenforceable.

9. The Emerald City Library

    A. The ECL or its representative has the right to make reasonable inspection and review of the art piece and the progress of the work on reasonable request. The Artist must make the piece available for viewing if such request is made.

    B. The Artist acknowledges the ECL ownership of the piece during the time it is in their possession and ECL's use of the images of said piece through June 1, 2006 which ECL agrees to use in a suitable and tasteful manner in conjunction with promotion of the event.

    C. It is understood that any photographic image of the art piece, as well as the art piece itself will be accompanied by a credit to the artist.

    D. ECL retains the right to terminate this agreement upon 10 days written notice if the Artist is not at fault, or if the Artist refuses or is unable to complete the art piece for any reason.

A Fundraising Opportunity

*A compensation clause should be included if you to decide to offer one

10. This agreement constitutes the entire agreement between the parties and all terms and provisions will be binding on both parties and is governed by the laws of the state of Oz.

_____

Artist Name

_____

Address

_____

Phone

_____

On Behalf of ECL

_____

Title

What Your Artists Need From You

If you have a specific theme or design limitations these need to be explained clearly to your Artists and should be enumerated in the letter soliciting design submissions.

Your acceptance letter, which will go out to the Artists you select to participate, needs to reiterate the constraints. You need to remind them of when they will receive (or can pick up) their piece, when it must be returned, and any recommended materials to use for the

A Fundraising Opportunity

embellishment of the book.

You need to treat the Artists very well and let them know they are appreciated. Include them in all your promotional materials and always credit them as the creator of their piece whenever it is pictured or mentioned. They should receive any of the merchandise that might feature their work such as a postcard or poster. If you do a book or catalogue they should receive a copy. They should have two free tickets to all the events. The Artists are your stars.

Recommended Materials

The materials listed below have been found to work well on the fiberglass pieces. If having the books displayed outside the types of materials used are less crucial.

There are many materials that will work, I just urge caution and experimentation with glues and unusual finishes. The papier maché pieces can be embellished with just about anything!

Liquitex Acrylics
Golden Acrylics
West Systems or other high quality epoxy
Bondo or other auto body repair plastics

LaVergne, TN USA
19 August 2010
193947LV00002B/33/A